When I Asked The Learned Biologist

**Poems by
Mark Moberg**

The author wishes to thank the following people and institutions for making this dream come true:

Mary Carroll Moore and Idella Moberg for numerous editorial suggestions, and for trying to keep me upright as I learn how to skate across the slippery ice of creative literature.

Lynette Brannan, LB Productions, Becker, Minnesota, for her pleasing designs, attention to formatting detail and endless patience.

Sentinel Printing, St Cloud, Minnesota, for the quality of their product and the efficiency of their service.

ISBN Number: 978-0-615-35205-3

Table of Contents

The Appeal to a Higher Authority   7

To Be Continued   8

The Eyes Have It   9

Charley's Song   10

The Trees of Life   19

Who's the Oldest One of All?   21

The Dark Side of Kahil   22

A Small Piece of History   24

Telling History   26

World Tour   27

Banished   29

The Assumption   33

The Cabin   35

Origins   39

Lost   41

Polishing Rocks   41

Not the Last Word   42

Moving the Moral Furniture   43

From Hair to There   44

The Animal Shouter   47

Hymn to My Wife   52

When I Asked the Learned Biologist   53

Grace Before Dessert   61

The Laurel and Hardy Prayer   62

The Will of the Wind   62

Three Sons   63

Bragging Rights   63

That Spiritual Gift   64

Being Hated   65

Free(Way) Thinker   66

Grace   70

Undercover   71

Time Out   73

Friends   75

It Was a Crow   76

Duty   84

The Analysis   86

The Prodigal Son of a Bitch   87

Loss of Control   90

Multiple Parallel Heavens   92

On Being Late   94

POEMS

THE APPEAL TO A HIGHER AUTHORITY

When we are young the argument from authority goes

   like this:

"YOU'RE going to get a SPANKING,"

And

"I'M going to TELL!"

But when we are older and sophisticated we advance

   to:

"PEOPLE like you are REALLY stupid,"

Countered by

"YOU'RE going to go to HELL."

TO BE CONTINUED

There are too many discontinuities

Between myself and my brain,

Between music and noise,

Between a rock and a tree,

Between an ape and me.

There are too many parallel lines:

Freedom and necessity.

The finite and infinity,

Strength and vulnerability.

Show me where they all interweave

And then I will believe.

THE EYES HAVE IT

"The sky is the daily bread of the eyes,"

   Said Emerson.

If this is true, then the yellow of lillies

Is an addicting drug for the eyes,

Red begonias are the strawberry ice cream of the

   vision,

And the sight of purple salvias glowing at dusk

Is the cappuccino of the soul.

Since one God or another

Rolled together dirt, water and air,

And transformed that foamy brown mud

Into such a satiating rainbow feast of colors

And youth restoring fountains of perfume,

Then it may be the case

That gardening is the most divine form of meditation.

CHARLEY'S SONG

I can hear in my mind the instruments

contentedly doing their work,

The soft cutting of scissors through compliant tissue,

The dull click of hemostats

Opening and closing on misbehaving arteries,

The intermittent satisfied gurgling of the suction tip

As it finds another pool of blood and saline

Making untidy its abdominal domain.

And most of all, the quiet murmur of small talk

Insignificant words, but each one holy in this place

Compared to the tense requests of the surgeon

And then the deepest silence

If only death and sorrow had been found within this
     incision.

They are putting Charley back together.

Charley is only a rag doll now,

His anatomy frayed,

His blood wandering off from its accustomed paths,

His bodily infrastructure riddled with shrapnel.

Slowly the surgical team reunites one part to another,

Lopping off something here, rerouting something

there,

Removing the interior body jewelry

Air-mailed to Charley

By people on the other side of a line.

From the skillful hands of the surgeons

Charley is passed to gentle nurse's hands

Who truss him and turn him,

Wrap him and unwrap him,

And baste him with care, affection and respect,

Until he's is done to perfection.

The army sends Charley home.

Only the mirror sees his scars.

He's a hero for a week.

After that only what has been retained

In his body and his mind

Speak to him of war.

Charley drinks too much and talks too little.

He is wise and he is foolish.

He is a hard worker and he is careless.

He meets up with Maxine, his high school girlfriend.

They circle each other warily for a few rounds,

And then fall into each other's arms.

Then, once again, life overcomes death:

Robert, John, Karen, David,

And finally little Gretchen.

Charley works two jobs.

For years his life is a Vivaldi concerto of dressing,

Undressing, diapers, leaky faucets, mowing, shoveling,

Playing catch, fixing doors, planting gardens,

Changing light bulbs, building playhouses,

Repairing the car, hugging, getting mad,

Being happy, paying bills, and being tired

(Which you yourself probably know well).

But five little angels drive out Charlie's demons.

As the children get older Charley's life

Acquires the drama of a Beethoven symphony.

There are ball games, school conferences,

Helping with homework, the facts of life,

Plays, concerts, vacation trips,

Encouraging, threatening, exhorting and comforting.

They must have done well

Because Charley and Maxine raise five beautiful
children,

Each more clever than the last.

And their children grow up with no serious problems,

Almost.

As he got older Charley became quieter.

Even though Charley was smart,

He was not a teller of stories.

But he knew how to listen, and he knew how to
laugh.

His grandchildren would skip with happiness
on the way to his house,

Their backpacks filled with their new jokes

And the stories taking place in their young lives.

Then they skipped with joy on the way home,

Their backpacks filled with the assurances

That they were smart, good looking and loved,

And still had some more of Maxine's cookies

That they could eat when they got home.

Finally Charley and Maxine

Are able to slow the pace to a Strauss waltz

As they drift down the broad river of a life,

Of being much valued for his wisdom and experience

    in the workplace,

Of respect and admiration in the community,

Of good friends, dining out, and traveling.

But some rivers, as they approach their end

Narrow and quicken

And must first flow through gorges,

And over waterfalls

Before they are gathered together

With all rivers

In the vast unencompassed ocean.

When Maxine began her descent into Alzheimer's

Their life capsized, and Charley was swept

Over rapids and into whirlpools.

It was exhausting to keep them both afloat

And the strange currents of her disease

Kept Charley bound down.

But he remembered every word they spoke

Whether in love, affection or impatience

Because he knew every word

    was also saying good-bye.

Letters, lists, check books and keys were lost.

Hidden reservoirs of patience

And grim determination

    were found.

Even the ticking clock on the mantel became erratic

As the months were lived by the hour

Or sometimes by the minute.

There were short periods of calm

And small acts of grace

That kept him sane.

The bond between them tightened and loosened,

But finally Maxine was swept away from Charley's

    grasp

And into the nursing home.

She died three weeks later.

Charley stays in their house.

He cooks, he does the laundry,

He vacuums, he gardens, he mows,

And as he wanders from room to room

He talks to her,

A different conversation for each room.

The worst time, he says, is at night.

Dreams of the war have returned to him.

He wakes up agitated.

He gets up to pee,

And still half asleep, returns to their bed.

He can never get over that she's not there.

So he cries alone.

I can hear in my mind the surgeon's tools

    quickly attacking flesh.

The soft sigh of a scalpel quickly drawn,

The sharp click of hemostats closing on tissue

    in rapid succession,

The continuous loud slurping of the suction tip

And most of all, the terse rapid naming of instruments

"Mosquito, mosquito, sponge, MORE EXPOSURE,

   MORE EXPOSURE,

Cautery, mosquito, more suction, shit, mosquito,

Sponge, mosquito, Jesus Christ!"

Chances are that for this kindly old man

An abdominal aneurysm is the end.

But it's not.

I lied, of course.

Charley is just a picture in a frame

On a spinet piano

In a living room,

And although the occupants of the house

Are forty years older than the young man in the

   picture

They still refer to him as "uncle,"

This handsome young soldier

Whom they never knew.

This whole fantasy is written out

Only as a small way of showing respect for Charley

By trying to do with paper and ink

That which those who loved him

Could only do with their tears:

By trying to imagine

What might have been.

THE TREES OF LIFE

Some children are like acorns.

They fly off the branch

Heading for the nearest ground,

Announcing their landing

With a satisfying kerplunk.

They are reliable, predictable

And as comfortably dependable as oak furniture.

Other children are like maple samaras,

Enchanting us as they

Whirl and glitter in the sun,

Staying aloft for a while,

Enjoying their brief freedom

Before seeking out a suitable spot to take root

And fulfill their destiny.

Still other children are like cottonwood seeds,

Aimlessly floating one way

Then drifting off in another direction,

Endlessly staying airborne,

Keeping all options open.

Their final destination is unpredictable,

But they often find fulfillment

Near a running stream of creativity.

They think that their wanderings

Are entirely self directed,

But, as you yourself know well,

One can't feel the wind

If one doesn't have at least one foot on the ground.

WHO'S THE OLDEST ONE OF ALL

I have scrubbed my hands.

I am getting ready to be gowned and gloved.

I rapidly shake my hands to get them dry.

There is a mirror in this operating room.

I look in the mirror and see

An older surgeon slowly waving his hands.

At home in the morning when I wake up,

Upon looking in my mirror

I see my father

Getting ready to shave.

And some of my best friends,

When they wake up in the morning,

Look in their mirror

And see their father

Putting on make up.

THE DARK SIDE OF KAHIL

Some youths

In the springtime of their life

Plant carefully a forest of exotic trees

And then they marry someone with a chainsaw.

Some adolescents,

When their world is young and fresh

Raise exotic birds of beautiful plumage

And then they marry someone with a shotgun.

Some, newly wedded, plough, seed and compost

And husband their spouses like dirt

So they are sure to get only the crop they want.

Some couples, through the years,

Scatter so many land mines

Over the conversational terrain

That they have to hire professional help

To safely remove them.

But some newlyweds

Scatter seeds of wild flowers on their marriage

And then wait to see what comes up.

Other young people, when first they wed,

Put delectations on the bird feeder of their love

And then wait to see what winged jewels will appear.

So remember, marriage is not a game of GO

With blocks and slides and ladders.

Though your stratagems have facets that are brilliant

    yet subtle,

(All carried out in love, of course)

Your spouse may not admire them as much as you

    do.

But work your marriage like a mine

And when jewels are discovered

Put them on display in a case

And through them you and your spouse and the sun

Can look at each other.

A SMALL PIECE OF HISTORY
(dipped in wine)

A young father is walking his son.

The father walks with cockiness in one hand

And tenderness in the other.

The son hops on his left foot in adoration

And on his right foot in self-importance

They hold hands

And in that grip is a communion,

And a transmutation of elements

Because the young father is a boy becoming a man

And the son is a child becoming a boy.

In the intersection the stranger walks right into them.

In the collision the stranger drops his packages.

From the stranger we have curses, insults, shoving,

   a slap.

From the father we have retreat, apologies,

Groveling on the ground to retrieve the packages,

A smile given only as a humiliating ransom.

The other people in the intersection watch.

They are good people, like me.

They don't cheat, steal or lie.

They don't sell their bodies or abuse drugs or alcohol.

They don't interfere.

Now there is a separation.

The father and son walk back home.

But fatherly pride stays behind.

The hands still join

But the eyes stay apart.

Sometimes I notice a black man

With more grace, dignity and fortitude

Than I myself can ever possess.

I think, "This too is a communion."

When I listen to the spirituals they whisper,

"The elements have been transmuted;

One thing has been made into another."

When I listen to the blues or to jazz they shout,

"And now the blood has been changed back into
    wine."

TELLING HISTORY

The time is coming

When the common creed

Will be "Everyone does it,"

When the only free market

Will be in political patronage,

And the cost of being not dependent

Will be a crushing tax.

At that time an intrepid youngster

Will find hidden away

A cache of dusty old pages,

Carefully concealed from the cultural authorities,

Writings by authors with names like

Burke, Washington, Jefferson,

Adams, Hamilton, de Toqueville,

Lincoln, and DuBois.

Maybe, just maybe,

That young kid

Will take those crazy old ideas

And start a revolution.

WORLD TOUR

Right now, all over the world,

There are men having their incorrect thoughts

   removed

By sharpened knives and rusty sickles

Applied to their viscera and their genitals.

There are men of tribe or race forbade

Who are atoning for their defects by being filleted,

Or ministered to by a soulless man of conscience

   flawed

Who's an artist with a cattle prod.

And they pray for deliverance to their god.

Right now, in many earthly places

There are little children

Whose numbered breaths ahead

Are a lot less than the hairs remaining on their heads.

These children are at the end stages of a slow

   starvation

Or a disease whose treatment requires unaffordable

   renumeration.

Like burning coals upon one's soul are the ever

weakening cries

As in loving helpless arms a little child dies.

How would you like to carry that sadness

Forever in your eyes?

And they pray for deliverance to their god.

Right now, around the globe

In many darkened rooms

Women are being raped by some cretin

And being mutilated and beaten.

It is no comfort to these humans broken

That of their trials no word dare be spoken.

Few people care, and until her life's complete

In every eye humiliation she will meet.

And they pray for deliverance to their god

Stupid GOD.

Does he expect us

To be his hand and feet?

BANISHED

Once upon a summer morning

At the cabin's long and heavy breakfast table,

Crowded with family and friends

    of several generations,

The coffee was taken with stories,

The toast was buttered with religion

And the eggs were taken with politics on the side.

That morning I managed to have finger in everything.

I stuffed myself with debate,

With muffin crumbs dribbling out of one side of my

    mouth

And dogmatic certitudes out of the other.

I'm not sure if it was the many cups

Of an exceptionally dark roast

Or the confusion brought about in my mind

By having to decide whether to have

Wild raspberry jam or maple syrup

On my pancakes,

But I soon detected the sound

Of a syllogistic chain saw

On the back side of my flawless ideology.

As I tumbled down to the firm ground of fact

I was made aware that my current line of argument

was insulting four sitting relatives, three professions

And two major religions.

Therefore,

At the point of a fork

Still dripping with warm maple syrup,

I was made to walk the dock.

So down to the lake I went,

Walking to the end of the dock

Which, sodden with morning dew

Provided a wet walkway over the smooth water.

The nearby loons still greeted me with deep bows,

The crayfish raised their claws in adoration,

And the bass under the dock

Gave me possession,

Floating at attention

Ten feet away.

I prostrated myself

With my head over the edge of the dock

To survey what realm was left to me.

I grasped the minnow net

And prepared to perform an act of man.

My net swept through the water,

Its wide mouth eager to swallow

Whole schools of minnows,

But, enjoying this effortless game of tag,

They easily evaded the net.

Then, seeing a minnow swimming by itself,

I snuck the net up behind it

And captured it easily.

"Look here, you son of a spawner," I said.

"Doubtless you have very good ideas

And have valuable insights

That the schools you despise laugh at,

But look who's in the net

And look who's free."

"Even for a minnow,

Truth is a community property.

Everyone has some of it,

And no one has all of it.

Now go back and stay closer to your kin fish"

Just as I was turning the net inside out

My wife hallooed me from the deck

And beckoned me back to the table,

Where she kept my mouth so full of pancakes and
    bacon

That I couldn't say a thing.

THE ASSUMPTION

The sociological assumption is that everyone except

    sociologists

Behaves like a herd of cows.

The experimental psychologist assumes

That everyone carries on like a laboratory rat

    except for the psychologists themselves.

The economists think that all we humankind,

    economists excepted.

Are greedy individuals and life is about getting.

But that was yesterday's news.

Today, the economists say,

Your life is a game

And its all about betting.

The evolutionary psychologist assumes

That the rest of us all are behind the times

By about fifty thousand years.

And nearly every single paper published

By the scientists who study cognition

Seeks to show that animals think more

And humans think less

Than it appears.

Now make a thin book about everything

That science has changed

In the way you think

About human nature.

And make another book

about the mistakes and fads they have caused.

It will be a little bit thicker.

You will find very little in the first book

That a wise man wouldn't already know

Two hundred or two thousand

Years ago.

THE CABIN

We have to sell the cabin.

We have to sell the land.

No longer will blessings fall on my family

Like the patter of light spring rain on the cabin roof.

No longer will this land cradle my family's spirit

As the earth cradles the pond of clear water at the

    spring.

I go down to the beach to pull up the dock.

No longer will the giggling waves caress my grand-

    children.

The waves will be forever young and ready to play,

But my grandchildren will grow up

(And I will grow old)

Without them.

I back the truck into the driveway on a fall day.

The trees are necklaced with emeralds, rubies and

    gold,

But the smell of damp fallen leaves

Will no longer dance around the cabin

With the scents of beef, carrot and onion of my wife's
   cooking.

The kitchen table is taken apart and placed in the
   truck,
The table at which family stories were served,
Traditions were passed around
And the coffee was drunk and the cookies were eaten
   in remembrance.

One last time I let the ancient hunting trails swallow
   me up,
The trails on which fathers will no longer be followed
By sons in an endless procession
On paths that lead backwards in time
As far as you wish to walk.

I sit down on the west facing deck one more time.
I watch the same sky, the same water and the same
   old trees
That my grandfather and I used to watch while we
   were talking.

My grandfather grew up when children

Were not only loved

But completely indulged

With hard work, discipline and good manners

And were only rewarded

With periods of the unwatched, unfettered freedom

To be children, at least until supper time,

When people lived in communities,

When anyone with a simple pole always caught

    enough fish,

When no land was posted,

And when everyone knew exactly where their food

    came from.

When my grandfather

Sat on that deck and told stories

Even the clouds would move in closer to listen,

The birds at the feeder would cock their heads

And in the tree tops

The balsam would nod to the spruce in agreement.

We have to sell the cabin

To someone whose power and wealth

Now entitles him to this land and this cabin

Which has been the dwelling place

Of the soul of my family

For so many years

Here on the shores of Lake Gikitisiminan.

ORIGINS

Yield the right of way, beautiful automobiles.

Stay in your own airspace, graceful jetliners.

Stop blocking the sun. lofty sky scrapers.

Evolution is the supreme designer here,

Ruthlessly weeding out inefficiencies,

Deleting everything that does not meet her exacting
standards.

Evolution is a master of trying new tricks

And at the same time a genius at using what's at
hand.

You could fill an auditorium with doctors and
scientists

And each one would be an expert

On one of evolution's amazing innovations,

Or one of her miracles of making due with what's
available,

Living flagrantly within exacting limitations.

We are the children of evolution

But are we obedient and dutiful,

Or are we rebels.

Do we use our reason and morality to escape her

dominion,

Or are they just they her latest tricks

To keep us under her firm control,

To keep us from traveling beyond her universe.

If evolution were a goddess, I would taunt her

abilities;

"Why don't you do something about Genesis 3:16?"

Ms Evolution would just smile.

It's the one place where she and God happen to

agree

On how to discipline their rebellious children.

God punishes us for being arrogant

And Ms evolution punishes us

For having big heads.

LOST

Life can be a dense pathless forest

With brambles that scratch us

And insects that sting us

As we try to fulfill our lives.

Fortunate are those

Who have the compass of reason to guide them.

Comforted are those

Who can see a distant mountain of faith to lead them.

Blessed are those

Who have a great river of love to walk beside.

POLISHING ROCKS

Even though life can be a rock tumbler

In which we are scratched, beaten and hit,

Try to become the gem stone

Instead of being the grit.

NOT THE LAST WORD

The birth process lasted for generations,

And although there were many premature pains and

    false labors,

And even though it was a very difficult delivery,

Eventually one of our distant ancestors brought forth

With joy and pride and absolute entrancement

The first word.

Of course, nobody else knew what it was.

So there were days of parading it around

And endless pointing and proud smiling.

By and by other people in the tribe

    began to understand.

And everyone nodded and smiled

    and became more wise.

The second birth didn't take as long.

The delivery wasn't so difficult.

One day it just sort of popped out.

A man used the wrong word.

After the momentary silence

Do you think everyone laughed at this, the first joke?

Or do you think only one man laughed

And benefited from the first lie?

MOVING THE MORAL FURNITURE

Moving a moral standard

Is like moving a heavy piece of furniture

In an overfurnished room.

So before we pick it up

We decide where we'll put it down

Or we may end up with the dining room table

Sitting on the piano.

FROM HAIR TO THERE

What is evolution's non-design with the placement of
  our hair?
When we ourselves our skin examine, in some places
  the hair isn't there.
Is evolution's hair styling a sex allure affair,
Or such a survival liability that soon we'll all be bare?

A beautiful head of glistening hair is of a young girl
  the glory,
But does the really hairy armpit also have its own
  seduction story?
Or is our hair in islands shrinking in an advancing sea
  of skin.
The evolutionary validation of voyeurs everywhere?

Whence began the peculiar institution of shavery?
When our ancestors were more fully furred
One wonders where and why they first applied the
  blade.
Could walking crop circles once have indicated
A character more savoury?

Could once the poodle cut have been the height of
    fashion
For the primate maid?

Was it at first a declaration of divorce,
Or a barbery sign of being from the closet cleared
Or the mark of devotion to a monastic life revered
When first were cut short those convenient domestic
    handles,
The waist length tresses and the curly beard?

Coal plants have been reviled.
Processed foods our metabolisms have defiled.
The chemical industry has been called to account.
By the hair and beard industries are we too beguiled?

Through thousands of years of trial and error
Genes and natural selection,
The evolutionary holy writ,
Determined the length of hair and beard that would
    permit
The maximum survival and reproductive benefit.

What evolution has sewed together

Let not mankind unknit

When we take our skin for a walk

We hear the bark of the dog,

The squirrel's scold and the blue jay's squawk,

But maybe it's just animal laughter at the sight that

   we make,

The naked nerds of the animal kingdom,

Holding aloft our gigantic heads on spindly necks,

So proud of our tool use,

But all our fur is fake.

THE ANIMAL SHOUTER

On a quiet summer afternoon,

When it seems to have escaped everyone's attention

That I was unoccupied,

I took advantage of this unusual situation

To slip away and spend some time with Thomas
Jefferson.

When I finally got to the writing of the Declaration of
Independence

I found myself getting restless,

And so, taking my cue from President Jefferson
himself,

Since I already had life, and was, as I said, at liberty,

I decided to pursue some happiness

By going outside

To find myself some "Laws of Nature" and "Nature's
God."

Surely mankind's essence includes organizing as well
as thinking.

So I spread myself out on the cool grass,

Let the sun dapple my body with heat,

And I watched the ants.

When I observed their frenetic pursuit

    of ant appropriate ADLs

My own sloth and unproductivity became to me

As enjoyable as a heavy sweating mug of cold beer

With a thick froth of the most delicious guilt.

My laziness was interrupted.

I found myself colonized and tasted and irritated.

"See here, pinheads." I said in revenge,

"You are all nothing but slaves.

The phrenomes you all read so avidly

Are nothing but constructions of your ruling classes.

The nectar from the larva is the opium they use to

    control you.

There is no such thing as the divine right of queen

    ants.

When you die you are not going to an ant heaven

At the center of the earth,

And I am not an omen of the end-times."

I next walked down a country road.

Near the fence a cow was gently licking her calf.

She stuck her wet nose over the fence in a friendly
   greeting.
I offered a hand instead of a nose, but it sufficed.
"Well, Mrs Cow, you appear to love your calf.
Do you love the other cows, too?
Could you even love me?
If the occupants in the yonder prison
Were to suckle at your oxytocin laden teats
Would they too gambol peaceably in the green
   pastures"?

Next I encountered a wolf crossing the road ahead
   of me.
We looked into each others eyes.
What did we see?
A cautious intelligence?
A prudent bravery?
A very conditional respect?
"Just think," I said to the wolf, "If we could give you
   a human body
You could be even smarter."
The wolf pricked up his ears at this.

"You could be very successful

And you could use all of your wiles and cunning

To rise to the top of my very large pack.

You could be in business or politics or jail,

depending on your intelligence,

Because basically, you're a total psycopath."

The wolf pretended he wasn't listening

and trotted off.

Then I went to the zoo.

I looked into the eyes of the chimpanzee.

Did I see my own reflection?

Was I looking back in time at my own origins?

Was I looking at thoughtfulness, empathy, wonder?

Then he threw something smelly at me.

"Look you lazy evolutionary dead end,

You're nothing but tree trash.

Why don't you take your corrugated cerebral cortex

And your 99% human DNA and follow the example of

the ant.

Organize yourselves, build, create, cooperate.

Change the world, make your mark.

Leave something behind besides your own dung."

Righteous shouting is so exhausting,

So I drove back home

To indulge myself with a nap.

With President Jefferson on my breast

I dozed off, leaving the afternoon sun

To slowly explore the porch furniture.

All the different members of the animal kingdom

Moved themselves, each in its fashion,

Through my drowsy mind;

All that hierarchy, but no equality.

"Wherever you got your conception of human nature,

Mr. Jefferson," I mused,

"You must have thought the human species

Was something more than just another animal."

Then I slept like a cat.

HYMN TO MY WIFE

When I survey my wondrous wife

Who staked youth and beauty on a "yes,"

To the most important question of my life

I am again amazed at the gift that I possess.

With an amazing a reserve of mental balance

She put much of her identity in escrow

While composting her own considerable talents

So that others might thereby grow.

Who wants to marry a poet

As a reality show will never arise.

If you're tempted by a poet, you'd better forego it

They see with their ears and hear with their eyes.

Now as we walk down this unfamiliar path

Through the valley of the shadow of our growing old

I would count it as my richest gain

If she would consent my hand to hold.

WHEN I ASKED THE
LEARNED BIOLOGIST

When I asked the learned biologist

About how we came to be

This is how she solved the mysteries

And explained myself to me:

"Your body is a walking, talking chemical factory

Within the bounds of your skin.

Hundreds of chemicals it daily makes

Whose molecules around each other spin.

In a ballet so complicated and intricate

It could drive a chemist to gin."

I was impressed. I was surprised.

"My body's a miracle. What can it mean?"

"Don't get metaphysical," she said.

"It's just a machine."

Then she showed me the fateful meeting

Of sperm and egg

Each has what the other needs.

The frantic sperm tries to enter

The gigantic object of its desire.

The egg at last concedes.

The passion of the two tiny cells explodes

Into growth along an exponential line.

From one cell, two, then four, then eight;

Two to the power of forty nine.

Groups of cells scurry from here to there,

Bringing in new building materials,

And carrying the trash away

Pulling out the right biochemical tools to build their

    part,

According to the plans in their DNA.

The embryo becoming a fetus

Has identity issues to negotiate

Or else a sense of humor genetically innate.

First it's a fish, then it's a frog

Then it's an alien from outer space.

But sparing its parents too much distress,

arms and legs it acquires

And even a face.

Transformer toys are very clever
But with the human fetus they do not compare
It's as if the city of New York itself had built
Without any humans being there.

I was astounded. I was amazed.
"Surely this is evidence of intelligent design."
"It is driven by the laws of chemistry," said she.
"There is nothing about it that's at all divine."

"The embryo", said she, "
"before it forsakes the womb
Over millions of seconds itself transforms
In ways extremely profound.
Just so the species
changes in form, shape and size
over millions of years of time unwound
and even divides."

"Surely this shows signs of an intelligent plan ," said I.
"Too many idiosyncracies and inefficiencies," she
    replied.

"Like in Microsoft Word?," was my aside.

"The next item on our agenda,"

Said my artful guide, still in very fine form,

"Is to take the brain itself by storm."

"The brain is an analogue computer

Thousands of inputs on its surface reside

With massively parallel processing inside."

"The brain is also a library of associations

That the brain notices

Between things that happen

Close together within time's pace,

Or within close proximity in space."

"The brain is a drug den in which one finds

Gangs of cells that drugs are craving.

They make the body move its arms, legs and mouth

Like a puppet that on a string is slaving.

The neurons make the body do what it needs

To get the food and sex and strokes and praise

That will let these tiny drugged out master cells

Stay in their neurotransmitter daze."

"From this three pound glob of drug laced jello

Where we keep our id and ego

Comes everything I am,

Everything you might be,

All of our culture,

And even all of history."

I laughed in amazement at this whole affair.

"What one couldn't do with dirt, water and air.

If we have a big enough pot

And give it enough time

The laws of chemistry will make them combine.

And sooner or later,

If some comet doesn't blow it,

We'll look in that pot and see life as we know it."

"It's as if you took your computer off line.

Wrote a few pages of code, maybe eight or nine,

Started an "if-then" a dozen times nested,

And then went to the beach for a week and rested.

Upon your return while you're eating lox on a roll

Your screen turns on and begins to scroll:

The plays of Shakespeare now are there,

The symphonies of Beethoven and all of Voltaire,

The architectural drawings for the Burj Khalifa Dubai,

The Gettysburg Address and the number pi,

The odds for next year's Super Bowl

And twenty five informercials on weight control.

Even God would be impressed

'Not too bad for one day's work and six of rest.'"

"Now," she said, "you're just being sarcastic,

In a tone of voice that doesn't fit you well.

Why can't you just accept

The wonders that science has to tell?"

"Why is it." I asked,

(Did I mention that her eyes were blue?)

"That you who are so curious

And so non-judgmental, too

(except toward those who believe ID is true)

And, in spite of your skepticism, also so kind,

Do not allow others the same freedom of mind

To look with doubt at some ideas you hold

That directly contradict the world they behold?"

"Well," she said,

As her hand upon my arm she gently lay,

"You have only one life to live

And for the present day

you can live it in reality,

Or under your imagination's sway,

But sooner or later,

reality will have its way."

"But," I said, trying very hard to frown,

(Did I tell you that her hair was brown?)

"In your fields you till for understanding.

Greed and self-centeredness are as real as rocks,

But under the sunlight of your investigations

An altruism that has no thought of any reward

Is shown to be a word of no meaning

And evaporates like the dew.

As I gaze into your eyes

That hardly seems like you."

With her seductive smile thus she did object:

"For the sake of passing on our genes

Our brains are hard wired

To make connections, relationships inspect,

Draw conclusions, infer cause and effect.

Sometimes we create meanings

When there is none at hand,

In the brighter light of science

Such meanings cannot stand."

As she steadily returned my gaze

She also took my hand.

"Why is it," I persevered,

"That as we rest together in the shade of the tree of

life

Admiring all its forms and colors

Where you see complex biochemical interactions

I see signs of an intelligent purpose.

Where you see the result of an inevitable chain of

events

I see an improbably unique occurrence

And where you see blind chance, I see a miracle"?

Her reply quite knocked me all askew

And changed my life forever.

I saw the world through glasses new,

Her answer was so clever.

"In our differing views", she said, "of what is true

The answer is quite simple, there's nothing amiss.

It's just that I'm a little smarter than you."

And she gave my cheek a kiss.

GRACE BEFORE DESSERT

The Lord bless you and keep you.

The Lord make his face to shine upon you.

The Lord lift up his smile upon you,

And give you a big piece of the pie.

THE LAUREL AND HARDY PRAYER

Well, (God), here's another fine mess you've gotten us
    in.
The ice we're skating on is pretty thin.
This isn't exactly a green pasture, you know,
There might be another way to make our faith grow.
But we trust we'll soon be able our thanks to pray
For delivering us from the trouble that we're in today.

THE WILL OF THE WIND

The wind blows where it wills.
Who can tell from where it's blowing
And who can say where it is going?
Does the pushing out of one place it compel
Or being pulled to another place in which to dwell?
And how could we tell?

THREE SONS

There was a man who had three sons.

One morning he said to the sons,

"Go out into the world and work today."

The first son went and tried to be righteous.

The second son went and tried to be obedient.

The third son went and tried to be useful.

Which of the three sons did what his father wanted?

BRAGGING RIGHTS

Of your spiritual gifts do not brag,

Neither of thought nor deed nor letter.

God's attention it will attract

And he might try to make you better.

THAT SPIRITUAL GIFT

I know I have a dark side.

I could find it without a light.

It's at the bottom of the basement stairs,

The first door on the right.

I've never actually unlocked the door.

It's not that I don't care.

I've looked through the keyhole once or twice.

There's really not much there.

It really is a burden,

Being so morally insightful.

People treat you differently,

Like they're jealous or even spiteful.

I'm never selfish with my wisdom

As I point out things they cannot see

Which are so obvious to everyone else,

But especially to me.

But do you think they show any gratitude

When I pop their narcissistic bubble?

It's such a thankless task I'm given.

I don't know why I take the trouble.

And sometimes when I really hit the mark

And knock off their precious crown

Their failings they try to project on me

So I just have to slap 'em down.

BEING HATED

If you're convinced that you've got to be hated

And all for the sake of His Holy Name

Try to arrange that you be berated

By the right and the left exactly the same.

FREE(WAY) THINKER

Procrastination is my only Godly virtue.

One advantage of being so consistently late

Is that I become a sociologist of the tailgate.

When to two lanes in my direction I am confined

Which car do I not want to be behind?

A car to avoid, if you can,

Is the rusting larger old sedan

That goes down the road bobbing like a boat

Carrying a family doing its best to stay afloat.

A "Truth in bumper stickers" law

might stick these cars with

"Give us this day our daily miles,"

Or "We've made mistakes, we've had our trials."

In contrast to the brand new BMW

(No problem following this car)

Whose bumper sticker might confess "This I deserve."

Smoking drivers you should try to pass by.

Juiced on nicotine, you'd think they'd just fly

But loafing along in their ashtrays on wheels

They're not in a hurry, they're enjoying the high.

Pick-up trucks can slow you down even more,

Even shiny black cabs-and-a-half with four on the

    floor,

Jewels that no one would ever dream of taking off

    road

Or ever risk scratching the bed with a load.

Pickups with toppers are the slowest of all.

I've never seen even one that didn't just crawl.

Have they all been there and done that

And now they have nowhere else to go,

Or were they wise enough in their youth

To set their life's goals just a little bit low.

But maybe there's something fragile under the topper,

Or perhaps something else very improper:

Elvis on velvet to sell on the street,

A wedding cake he made for his daughter sweet,

A crop of marijuana he grows on the side,

Or somebody's body he's trying to hide.

There is a narrowing right after a stop light

On my daily to the workplace ride

Where the road abruptly drops to two

Instead of being four lanes wide,

And although we all merge

By our driving behavior we also divide.

For some the order of arrival

    is the most important thing.

Taking a back seat are relative speed

    and the common good,

And those who see behind the rules,

    they never understood.

But then there are some young drivers

    who cheer up my soul

They can easily intuit each other driver's

    immediate goal.

If I drive a little faster I can just squeeze in;

Get as many through before the light turns red.

If we make room for each other, we'll all get ahead.

Driving in line by the government center

At just barely over five miles an hour

It's easy to think of our political divides
And my thoughts turn dour.

Socialism is a two lane highway
The slowest car is at the head of the line
With a trailer of entitlements pulled behind
To remark upon which you'd best decline.

Capitalism is a freeway where you don't have to
    queue.
What you accomplish is up to you.
Energy and ideas receive their reward,
But everyone benefits before they're through.

Unregulated capitalism is a freeway where no rules
    reign
Greed is not harnessed for society's gain.
Cheating and lying blow everything away.
The rich and the poor are all that remain.

Finally I park
When my drive to work reverie is complete.
My sense of entitlement,
My misdirected rage,

And my insecurities replete

I try to remember to leave on the seat.

GRACE

When I want to feel like a boy again

I lie myself on the river bank

And look down at the mighty Mississippi.

Thousands of gallons of water per second,

A silent but unstoppable force,

Southward flows.

Then I roll over and look above me

Where the cumuli, standing in lines

Waiting for a wind,

Are the only visible signs

Of that equally great river in the sky

That northward blows.

UNDERCOVER

Mr. Perkins was a man who could walk tall and erect.

He had the love of his wife and his children's respect.

He had the trust of his boss and a circle of friends.

That he had oppressed so many you'd never expect.

His wife, at least outwardly, seemed content with her
   station.

She received flowers and jewelry on every occasion.

They went out for drinks, and had long talks

And were frequently seen taking walks.

If you didn't really know him you'd have no clue

That he was a redneck racist and sexist, too.

He often listened to the news on NPR

Stories of sadness in lands afar,

Starvation of children and terrible disease,

Civil distress and private armies,

Separating of limbs with bright metal blades,

Cutting off heads and throwing grenades.

Seeing him live quietly in his modest home

You'd never guess at the mischief he'd sown.

And so it appears that this upstanding fellow

If he had a conscience at all, it was really quite

    shallow.

He wasn't contrite, he wasn't uncertain

He didn't seem to know about the white male's

    burden.

TIME OUT

To the monks of St John's and the nuns of
   St. Benedict's

I sometimes consider with satisfaction

The 64 years with which my life is crowned

But then I remember that for 13 billion

I wasn't even around,

And then when I'm gone

For how many billions more will I not be found?

So it really seems, considering the aforesaid,

That my natural state is being dead.

What a sad thought, I said with a pout.

I must find some way

To stretch my remaining years out.

So between the goal posts of my life

I have marked out the twenty minute lines

At which to think a prayer about the fate

Of someone that I love

Or even hate.

And if I live too fast

And get to thirty or forty five

I still stop to look around and say

"Isn't it great to be alive."

FRIENDS

I have friends who could have been models,

Authors, actors, rock musicians

Entrepreneurs, CEOs, beloved physicians,

TV personas, sharp legal minds,

Richest four hundreds, experts of all kinds,

Scientists famous, inventors renown,

Movers, shakers, talks of the town.

The reasons they aren't are quite common enough:

Parents too soft, or parents too tough,

Bad habits, bad luck, growing up in a cocoon,

Bad education, wrong crowd, being born too soon,

Wrong place, wrong time, not enough greed,

Not enough energy, wrong values received,

Not enough questions, not enough "Why's?"

Way too much free time, believing in lies.

But if they had been among the (mis?)fortunate few

Who achieve fame and fortune, maybe happiness, too,

Who they are now they would not be,

And they certainly wouldn't have time for me.

IT WAS A CROW

Once upon a midnight dreary

While I struggled weak and weary

Over many an unpaid bill and threatening letter,

I pondered how to continue my financial balancing

    act,

And I could not help but cursing at being such a

    debtor.

"What were you saying?" a gravelly voice asked

As I was swearing at my dismal task.

Startled, I looked around the room

Where I thought I had been drinking alone

From my private bottle of misery.

On my eye's second tour around the room

I saw the crow standing in the door ajar.

With tiny brown glasses he looked quite bizarre.

He was smoking a small cigar.

"I asked you what you were saying."

"I was praying."

"Close enough." was the crow's reply.

Again I turned back to the task I abhorred,

Catalogues of stuff I couldn't afford.

Humiliated and stressed, my life I deplored.

Mountains of junk mail never read,

Letters from giant corporations who wanted my head.

I pretty much wished that I was dead.

Then the crow flew over me through the air.

A shower of ashes fell on my head.

He gently alighted on my best armchair.

"And who do you say that I am?" he asked

"Jesus Christ!!" I heard myself swear

As I threw my checkbook at his head.

"Close enough," was what he said.

"Why don't you come outside

Cool off, and cut yourself some slack,"

Said the crow, in the middle of his glide,

As he flew out into the night air so black.

So I followed this feathered unearthly guide,

Part of me hoping we'd never come back.

"What do you see?" asked the crow

With one wing strangely angled to the sky.

"I see stars, burning white hot in the darkness
Following their own purposes in their ceaseless
    circuits,
And like the interests of the powerful men
In distant places who control our futures,
Remote, indifferent and unchangeable.

I see the blackness of infinite emptiness
 Like my life, mirthless
And like my troubles, endless."

"Exactly," said the crow.
"Out there it is all empty space
for millions of light years in every direction
Except for a few lonely rocks
Dark, cold, hard and lifeless,
Drifting unseen through the blackness
Or an occasional distant beam of nuclear fire
Where molecules congeal and then expire
Before they are able to life conspire."

"But look at you.

Compared to what's out there

You are a marvel of biological beauty and complexity,

A miracle of thought, feeling and intention.

Nowhere else in that endless universe

Will you find someone like yourself

Who can speak a language,

Subtract and add,

Hang a frame, fix a door,

Use a computer,

Recommend your favorite brews,

Tell the stories that your friends amuse,

Tie your shoes."

"Even now your deep despair

Shows your dreams and how much you care,

Of what might have been and yet could be,

Dreams that you'll never find out there."

"No doubt," I argued, "in some other solar stardom

There is a life form of intelligence awesome

Who would really find my talents really tiresome."

"Supposing you were to go in a shuttle,"

Said the crow, still holding that cigar in his talons,

"To shine your instruments into the void

Looking for a place for that life to hide."

"Supposing your shuttle exploded

Sending you and your luggage

On an endless silent special journey."

"If there did happen to be another intelligent life form
    out there

Isolated, like us, on their rare inhabitable planetary
    jewel.

They would have history books like us,

Don't you think?

And on the timeline of their recorded history,

At the bottom of the page,

The biggest mark and pride of place

And even written in boldface

Might be the day YOUR dirty underwear

Floated in from outer space."

Then the crow gave me a pair of wings

And we flew around the globe

To a beautiful park of grass and trees

Around a small pond arranged

Presently occupied by the mentally deranged

They were rubbing against trees

Rolling on the ground

Running wildly around,

Or just staring at the sky spellbound.

"If I had the misfortune

To misplace my mind

And in searching for it

my behavior became a little queer

I wouldn't mind being put in here."

"They're not crazy,

They're just dead,"

He said

"They've been lying in their graves for years

Waiting for the resurrection.

We find them a body to use

Bring them here to do what they choose

And say 'fifteen minutes.

No time to lose.'"

"Can you imagine

When you've come back from the dead

A single touch is like a glass of ice water in the desert,

Seeing a bright color is like a cold lake on a hot day

And seeing a human face

Is like eating a pancake with butter and syrup

in the middle of a famine.

They are receiving a downpour of these sensations

Every single second.

In their fifteen minutes of ordinary bodily sensations

More intoxicating pleasures will they feel

Than you in the next fifteen years

Will ever find time to steal."

Then the crow picked me up again

And returned me to my troubles.

He took a slow puff on his cigar

Looked around, then said,

"You think about it, son,

And I'll stop by again in a few years

To see how you're doing."

Then his flapping wings lifted him into the air

And gracefully gaining altitude in an arc

He disappeared into the dark.

My life is still mostly trampled ground

The site of futile strategies in a losing battle.

Frantically I prop up the sagging beams of my

    existence.

Desperately I chase my life's dreams

Which elude me like frightened rabbits.

But sometimes I walk slowly, deliberately, head erect,

Letting the movements of my body bathe my mind,

Letting my eyes finger everything in sight

And letting myself be surprised, if in a public aisle

I get an unexpected return on a very shy smile.

Sometimes when I am performing

One of those endless menial tasks of maintenance

That only gets one somewhat less behind

But not one little bit ahead

I find myself saying

"Well, I guess you can't do this when you're dead."

Sometimes a park bench becomes the frame of a

    picture

Into which, I, as a child, wished to disappear.

I allow myself a short rest on the banks of my life,

And again I wonder, where God has hidden all his

    rainbows

And there once again I sometimes talk to crows.

DUTY

I know poor people

    who are happier than the wealthy.

I know slow people

    who are more cheerful than the smart.

I know great sinners

who are more content than the righteous.

How do they do it? Simple.

They cheat; they're lazy; they're selfish.

They refuse to do their part.

They've taken off the knapsack and kicked it over the

cliff.

They've taken off their heavy boots and they're

wading in the surf.

They say it's above their pay grade.

"Well," I say, "Be that way then.

But remember,

There are still some of us

Who can be depended on,

Who still will remain faithful,

Who will not abdicate

Nor our righteous passions ever stem

In our duty to criticize,

Our obligation to judge,

And our responsibility to condemn."

THE ANALYSIS

Sometimes to analyze is to destroy.

Have you ever read a funny book explaining humor

Or a creative book about being creative?

When we have come to totally understand

The biological foundations of morality

Will we all have amoral life?

Should we start with the simple things

Like the pattern of our cerebral wiring

when we hear a Beethovan symphony,

Or reverse engineering from the state of our neuronal
    net

To the words on the pages of Shakespeare?

Because when we move on to the study
    of consciousness

And can explain it all with ease,

We may all become as unconscious as a cheese.

THE PRODIGAL SON OF A BITCH

A certain wealthy man had two sons begot.

Each tried to be what the other was not.

The older son was thoughtful and smart,

A quiet blessing to his father's heart.

The younger son's misfortune lay

In that he was handsome and charming

And quite irresistible in a certain way.

So all through school a merry life he led

And was voted most likely to be shot

In someone else's bed.

But his father to his faults was blind

So he sent him out West himself to find

With a rather large slice of their financial pie,

Saying "certainly he will turn out as good as I."

Our younger son indeed did well.

He became a rock star singing songs from hell.

He was rich and famous and had women to spare.

It would have been best if the story ended there.

He became even richer by cheating his pals

Out of all their money and even their gals.

But then his howlings fell out of favor,

As even he drew the line at certain behavior.

Then he fell in with the usual thugs

And spent most of his money on sex and drugs.

Of the last of his fortune he was soon dispossessed.

His financial advisors had taken the rest.

As his purulent life came to a head

He finally wound up in a hospital bed,

Unclothed, unshaven, and covered with spit,

Wasted and weakened and smelling like disagreeable.

Late one night he woke up with a cry.

A beautiful nurse held his hand and asked "Why?"

"I saw an angel while I was dreaming,"

Said the prodigal son whose tears were streaming.

"And what did the angel have to say?"

Said the sweet young nurse, but in a professional way.

This was the message of the angel:

"You son of a bitch, there you lay

While your father still prays for you night and day.

Why don't you just admit you're a jerk,

And let your father's forgiveness do its work.

I can guarantee you that he will take you back

Restore your fortune and all that you lack.

You still have lots of talent indeed,

If you start singing gospel you're sure to succeed.

You'll not only be famous, if you answer His call,

But wealthy, respected and loved by all."

But he didn't go back, this prodigal son.

He was too proud to regret what he'd done.

A sanctified life he thought might be worse,

And besides, he thought he might make it

With the beautiful nurse.

LOSS OF CONTROL

Patients who are ill are sometimes said

To present with a constellation of symptoms

That points to a diagnosis.

Sometimes that diagnosis is itself a constellation,

Like Cancer, the crab.

But it is really in the wrong part of the night sky.

This disease belongs with the constellation Leo,

    the lion

Because cancer is a disease that stalks you.

You are skating through life

Thinking that because you're a good person

And because you don't have too many bad habits,

The lion will take the next person instead of you.

Even when you first feel the lion's jaws,

You don't believe it.

But then he shakes you until you're nearly dead,

Takes several large pieces of your precious flesh,

And drops you into a different world,

Where you acquire a whole new set of values.

Many mundane things become precious jewels.

And some relationships become closer than you

   thought possible.

Also there are certain people who talk too much

Whom you no longer have to listen to,

And other people whose agendas

You no longer have to pursue,

Because finally your time is more precious than theirs.

Then they give you the poison.

"Drink this. When the lion comes back,

Maybe the poison will kill him

Before it kills you."

MULTIPLE PARALLEL HEAVENS

I believe in the theory of multiple parallel heavens

At which not only will we meet our loved ones

   passed

But ourselves at a younger age,

Before our fate in the web of time stuck fast.

Ourselves as earnest little children,

Trying so hard to please,

Before the time we learned the art

Of how to lie and how to tease.

Ourselves we'll meet again as young adults

With both integrity and dreams to spare

Before we compromised ourselves

To make sure we got our share.

We will meet ourselves as we might have been

If at home, at work and play,

We had been able to look in other's eyes

Without our own needs getting in the way.

Had seized with entrancement and with pleasure

This gift of life which once was precious

Rather than primping and posing at our leisure

Waiting for life's desires to enmesh us.

Had been more attentive to quiet cries for help

Of those whose lives we might have saved,

Had been more interested in discerning

What others sometimes didn't say.

We will meet once more

That person we might have been

If we had not been so led astray

Nor did those things of which we never speak

Nor did the trust betray.

Perhaps in some younger selves

We felt weakened by being too forgiving,

Embarrassed by our generous side

And foolish by being so kind,

But to what kinds of voices were we listening

When we killed those better parts of us

And left them all behind?

ON BEING LATE

When I for the last time am about to be late,

Nervously awaiting my appointment with the grave,

With God I will renegotiate my fate,

Postponing death's close and claustrophobic cave.

"Please God, I can't believe my life is spent.

Might I just one more season of life regain?

Just one more night in my cozy tent

Listening to the patter of a summer night's rain?"

"Please God, these tightening bonds of death unlock.

The drapes of life are so quickly drawn.

Just grant me time to take one more walk

On a quiet ocean beach at dawn."

"Please, let me have just one more time

To sit with friends at a street café,

To talk and laugh and remember life

And sip the night away."

"Send me my grandchildren unto me.

Their faces I long just once more to see.

My children by my bed must stand

They must be here to hold my hand.

And don't think I am about to go anyplace

Until I feel once more my wife's embrace."

And God will say,

"I see that your memories are packed

With all those blessings that I did once bestow.

Now hold my hand; are you ready to go?"

And I will say

"Dear God,

At a time like this

Why do you make me smile so?"